FIRESEED

I dedicate this book with all my love
to my children, Amanda and Philip,
to my grandchildren, Jeremy, Becky, Thomas and Ferdy,
to my sisters Pamela and Rosemary
and to the 'Norah' of my poem

Clemency Emmet
1959

FIRESEED

poetry by
Clemency Emmet

paintings by
Elizabeth Cope

ARLEN
HOUSE

FIRESEED

is published in 2014 by
ARLEN HOUSE
42 Grange Abbey Road
Baldoyle
Dublin 13
Ireland
Phone/Fax: 353 86 8207617
Email: arlenhouse@gmail.com

Distributed internationally by
SYRACUSE UNIVERSITY PRESS
621 Skytop Road, Suite 110
Syracuse, NY 13244–5290
Phone: 315–443–5534/Fax: 315–443–5545
Email: supress@syr.edu

ISBN 978–1–85132–107–0, paperback

Typesetting: Arlen House
Printing: Brunswick Press
Cover images by Elizabeth Cope

CONTENTS

Clemency Near Window
oil on canvas
50 x 40
2014

Gillian Somerville-Large

Clemency Emmet writes about place with a dreamy precision. Her lively perception, pervaded with the charm of nostalgia, gives continued delight to the reader. In 'Lake House' we are taken among flags of white iris and mayfly, while 'Holiday with Norah' brings us to a white farmhouse with its turf fire, new-laid eggs and 'icy cold iron tasting'. She evokes her Californian childhood where she encountered 'glowing oranges' and spiders who threatened as 'fierce dragons'. In 'Pisces', sensibility drops the reader from the sunshine, following her fishing line and bait down to where the cannibal pike is waiting. From January marmalade 'bottling the sun' to the elaborate dance of the humming bird, the piano whose 'trills and scales' are beating like birds' wings, the beginning of love in 'Haymaking', and the sea's 'gentle stroking of the white beach' her language brings experience to life. She does not rely solely on memory, but on humour as well, particularly in her memorable poem, 'The Eightieth Birthday Present', which manages to combine a vivid description of the Florida mangrove swamps – crocodiles, Spanish moss, snakes and much else – with the satisfaction of reaching old age. Read her poetry with pleasure.

Dominica Pentecostes
oil on canvas
66 x 86
1997

WORDS

You choose words with utmost care,
conscious of their power.
In your hands they are tools
for good or evil.

To me your words are like small sparks,
golden in darkness.
Capable of bringing warmth and light,
speech that enchants.

Yet, too, your words can hurt,
turning into little tongues of flame.
Searching out my weakest places,
invading, searing my soul.

Today when you said goodbye,
no sparks burned.
The word stood ugly between us,
cold embers, no more to say.

Sandycove
oil on board
61 x 76
2004

SOLITUDE

I come down the path and you are there.
I wait until you have gone,
then stand in your place,
looking out over the lake,
perhaps thinking the same thoughts as you.

We both love the field where daisies grow,
and how it curves into a small hill
where distant beech trees stand.
I see you there sometimes, far away,
heedless in rain or sun.

You walk in the places that I love.
Could our two solitudes ever meet?

View of Kilkenny
oil on canvas
66 x 91
1996

SMALL TOWN

I know this town,
not as tourists know it.
I know the smell of these houses,
the stored history of the owners.
What they have to eat and when,
and what they talk about.

I know their cars.
The careful backing out of driveways,
the coats hanging in the hall.
How they sleep, in ones and twos,
in clean beds, good blankets,
waking up early, virtuous in work,
happy in holidays,
outraged at the unexpected,
inept in misfortune,
letting their children slip through their fingers,
unready for the outside world.

The children are fierce, they want to go
and yet they linger,
still looking over their shoulders
at warm-lighted rooms.

Texas Ranch (detail)
oil on canvas
196 x 75
2002

ORANGE RANCH CHILDHOOD

We played between walls of glossy leaves,
dark green, hung with glowing oranges
like lanterns in long fairy corridors.
Fruit and creamy blossom shared the branches
and childhood seemed to last forever.

Our fierce dragons, their spiders
invisible in shadowed depths of leaves.
In the early morning they spun their webs
which stretched like silver nets from tree to tree,
to trap unwary faces in their sticky veils.

On frosty nights the smudge-pots were lit,
warm, like toy stoves, between the rows of orange trees.
The thin lines of smoke rising in evening air
brought a calmness, a nursery quietness,
so that we accepted the winding down of day.

In the morning, wild again,
we gathered only the fallen oranges,
heavy and sweet. We savoured their over-ripeness,
the exhilarating taint
which spun in our heads like vintage wine.

Widow
oil on board
51 x 40
2006

THE WIDOW

I started life bare as a sapling.
Gradually my branches spread,
some crooked, some straight.
My roots grew far down,
I bore fruit.

For many a long year
I stood against wind and storm,
glorying in the weight of my leaves.
Children and children's children,
till loss cleft me.

I now am chilled as if by frost.
My trailing branches will not root.
Let me stay bare as I began.
There is less pain that way
for when I fall.

Dublin Airport
oil on board
56 x 71
2009

AIRPORT

I look for you
in all the faces going by.
I watch other people meeting
and wonder how they feel –
How will you feel?

You went away, you said,
to find yourself.
Now I do not know who you have become.

I have not changed,
I stayed here while you journeyed.
Unsure, waiting, missing you.

Will all your newfound expectations
shatter on the bare rock of my love?

from *Vauxhall Street Studio*
oil on canvas
56 x 76
2012

THE WHITE ROOM

Once I had a room in a high city tower.
The walls were painted white,
bare floor, a row of tall windows,
the minimum of furniture.
How cold, they all said,
how stark, no colour.
How can you live there?

But the light was like a benediction,
and the sky gave me its own colours,
luminous grey or brightest blue.
When the sun shone the air was gold,
filling the uncluttered room.
Sunset gave me rose and orange across my walls.
I had the silver glint of rain,
the soft shadows of snowfall.
Frost laid prisms of brightness at my windows.

There in my high city tower,
I was closer to the seasons
than many a country man.

Rabbits (detail)
etching
56 x 76
2012

HOUSES OF GORSE

Here are the houses of honey gorse,
where rabbits live in dusky rooms
with walls of twisted branches
and the slatted sun goes sideways in.

They lie in a long labyrinth
of light and dark, bodies pressed to earth,
eyes gleam in a rapt stillness
and overhead are flowering roofs of gold.

Arthur Wills
oil on canvas
46 x 38
1978

HUSBAND

Sometimes I can conjure up
a beloved ghost to walk beside me.
His strides as long as in his life,
happy, confident, shoulders back.
Smiling, gaze fixed on some far horizon,
I can match him, step for step.

Other times there is only silence.
Nothing to block the heartache of regret,
irretrievable days with words unsaid.
Comfort not given, sadness unrecognised,
yet, once, in my heart I heard you say
I remember only happiness.

Nest Negative
oil on canvas
244 x 372
2006

GRIEF

The picture was painted at his lowest ebb,
at the place where he thought he no longer cared.
Suddenly all his rage and buried sadness
came to life in one gigantic shout.
Out of his very depth the paint took form.
It frightened him to look.

Other people saw what was in it.
It surprised him that they could.
It achieved a kind of fame,
hung in the very newest of museums,
talked about, pushed into a 'movement'.
One day he went alone to see it,
found in a room marked 'Grief'.

For a long time he stood there thinking.
Paintings stretched away on every side,
different eras, different thoughts, different lives.
Could he still recognise his own cry, unique to him,
when here it became one more voice in a chorus?
His passion submerged in the fearful unity of grief,
he was just another stranger, lost in a crowded street.

Royal College of Surgeons
mixed media on paper
71 x 86
2013

THE STUDY GROUP

A third of the study group received true love,
another third were given placebos,
the rest, as control group, had neither.

Of those who were given true love,
some proposed, others lost their gift
through carelessness or lack of faith.

In the group that had only placebos
many never noticed what was missing
and led contented lives of make believe.

The control group, given nothing,
at first despaired, but then began to learn
their own true worth, of heart and mind.

Jeremy and Sybil (detail)
oil on canvas
152 x 304
2007

LONG AGO

I remember
sitting on the floor with two Frenchmen
discussing politics.
I wore orange silk and smoked Gaulois
because that's what one did then.

The image is vivid but so small,
like the bright screen of a drive-in movie
seen from far away.
Hollywood lights and sounds
bouncing off silent hills in darkness.

It was like that
but I still remember
the elation that filled me
being seventeen and still believing
that my words mattered.

Interior Rua Sao Gall Sao Paulo
oil on canvas
122 x 183
2014

SUNLIGHT

When you played the piano for us
the walls of the hospital retreated.
We danced on broken limbs.

You told us as a child
you played the piano with your father,
sweet mixture of music and love.
This you gave to all of us
like sunlight on a darkened day.

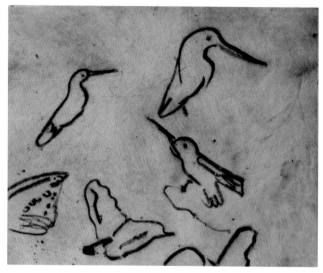

Humming Bird (detail)
etching
28 x 41
2014

THE HUMMINGBIRD

In childhood we never thought of dying,
we used time as if it never ended.
Now you are gone, and I remember
the long Californian days,
your joy in sun, in every flower and tree.

You loved the hummingbird's elaborate dance,
wings beating so fast they became invisible,
tiny brilliant body balancing on air,
searching for sweet hibiscus honey,
needle beak joined to open petals.

I saw you reaching out so gently,
for one long moment holding in careful hands
both bird and flower.

Barrie Cooke
oil on canvas
71 x 56
2009

THE PHOTOGRAPH

You stand four-square facing the camera,
feet together, hands stiffly by your side,
best clothes, polished shoes,
your expression arranged for the occasion.
This photograph was given to comfort me.
It makes you as distant as the stars.

In my mind you are untidy and laughing,
clothes awry, a joke on your lips,
expectation in your eyes,
full of joy and warmth.
In my memory you live and breathe.
This photograph can only document my loss.

Snow at Ekely, Norway
oil on canvas
56 x 71
2010

JANUARY

In the slow domestic rhythm of the year
January was the month of marmalade.
After the richness of Christmas
it came as a cleansing ritual,
the careful shredding of bitter oranges,
the sliding of sugar into the boiling pan.
Its golden heart lighting the winter day.
We filled the line of brilliant jars
as if, briefly, we could bottle the sun.

Farmhouse on Way to Killeshin
oil on board
61 x 76
1993

THE HOUSE

In the curve of the valley stood the house,
small, white, its pointed roofs aglow
with setting sun.
The world around it, mountains, sky and trees,
and far off the glint of the sea.

From the hills a path came down
one slender thread to the outer world,
skirting the house
beside it, yet no intrusion made
upon the self-containment of the place.

Here lived a man and a woman,
two alone, and all around them
animals moved through the woods and bracken.
Birds sang.
Trees and flowers grew, sun and rain came
and together the man and woman loved.

In the early mornings or now when the sun sets,
their love was like a fire in each.
The primitive tasks of sustaining life
became a holiness,
for all their life was love and their love, life,
and all was bound up in this.

With twilight the sky retreats and remote stars
come one by one to stop the blackbirds' song.
The tree branches take on darkness,
all is quiet,
the wind comes lonely down the mountains
and in the house is warmth and flame and peace.

Parrots, Parque das Aves (detail)
oil on canvas
61 x 186
2014

Return of Light

One Saint Lucia's Day, the Festival of Light,
one girl was chosen, always the most beautiful.
She had to be tall and strong,
like sacrificial maidens of old,
so that she could bear with dignity
the crown of lighted candles.

We watched as they were lit, one by one,
so close to her fine long hair.
She walked like a queen, her white dress flowing.
We followed her singing, but she seemed apart from
us,
her face transformed in the solemnity of candlelight,
holding a secret we could not share.

Only afterwards was she our friend again,
familiar, laughing. And the year had turned.

Trees in Shankill
oil on canvas
56 x 71
2013

PROGRESSION

She never saw how tall the trees had grown
or how she herself was so much smaller.
It took longer now to do her favourite walk,
going over the crest of the big field
down to a thick gathering of gorse and briar,
following rough paths forged by cattle
pushing their heavy bodies through the thorns.
Then she went into the woods, damp and cool,
where she would take rest
leaning against the mossy bark of trees.

She looked into layers of green leaves
going up and up towards the white sky.
The air so fresh and bright
that each breath was a satisfaction,
like quenching thirst.
The way back was uphill.
She took her time, busy with thoughts.
Memories hung all around her
like tattered old garments
which still clothed her, kept her warm.

Sheep on Turnips
oil on board
61 x 76
2009

FEED MY LAMBS

Feed my lambs, you said, Lord
but this woman is not a lamb.

She is more like a wild mountain ewe.
With her comes the bone-cold of the hills
and the feel of barren stony ground
where the only shelter is abrasive gorse
or the thorny clutch of the briar.

Her eyes show you this hard place.
Only the brutal ache of bare necessity
would bring her here in front of me.
Her outstretched hand is no gentle plea,
but a desperate unspoken threat.

O Lord, I did not feed your lambs,
for I gave in fear and not in love.

House in Roundstone
oil on board
124 x 154
2002

LAKE HOUSE

The house stands alone on a small island.
Around it the lake moves with the seasons,
rising to the wind, pinpricked with rain,
lying at rest in summer stillness.

Flags of yellow iris grow
among the palisade of reeds.
Wild duck nest and the mayfly spins,
blurring the edges of land and water.

Set between lake and sky,
this house belongs to either world.
When the moon lays a path across the water,
fish swim, dream-like, through the windows.

Joanna on Green Chair
oil on canvas
93 x 61
2013

RAPUNZEL

The wooden house stood above the shore,
four-square like a child's drawing.
The strong sea winds,
scouring with salt and sand,
had made its bare wood the colour of bone.

Nothing softened the stark outline,
except at one window, lace curtains.
Perhaps a girl lived there once
who hung the curtains as a challenge
to the bleak shore and the sea.

She would open the window and let the lace
billow out, luxuriant, catching the light
in its rich pattern of scrolls and flowers,
Like Rapunzel letting down her shining hair
saying 'here I am – this is me'.

Shouting against endless grey waves,
and the chill of the seagull's cry.

Giovanni on Bicycle
oil on canvas
81 x 64
2014

THE PORTUGUESE GARDENER

He worked better because the girl was there.
He trimmed and tended the small palm tree
until the base was a perfect pineapple shape
and the fronds a tidy green umbrella.
In the hot sun his shirt stuck to his brown skin,
he worked without stopping,
digging the earth around the tree,
kneeling to pull out weeds and stones,
running the clean earth again and again through his
fingers.

The girl watched silently, lovingly,
knowing the value of his work.
When he moved on she still stood there,
drawing strength from the ground he had tended.
She thought of his strong hands shifting the soil,
remembering his gentle fingers untangling her own
long hair.

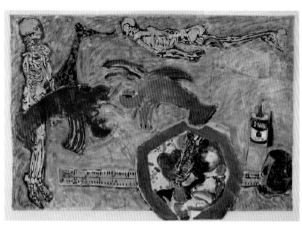

Nest Positive
oil on canvas
248 x 372
2006

SCORPIO

My daughter, visiting South Africa,
found a luxurious swimming pool.
Turquoise tiles, flowers in giant pots,
set in the middle of a wild game park.

The night before, young lions had visited,
knocking over the ornate pots,
playing games with trails of bougainvillaea
and stiff clumps of Birds of Paradise.

But now all was pristine and shining,
an oasis of tranquillity restored,
while in the distance dark shapes of elephants
followed the horizon like a fleet of ships.

There was a sudden flurry in the deep blue pool.
She saw three large insects struggling.
Using a giant leaf, she scooped them out,
laying them, one by one, exhausted on the bank.

As the hot African sun revived them,
she watched their tails curl slowly upwards,
revealing the dangerous venomous tips.
She had carefully rescued a trinity of scorpions.

Ballet on the Pond
oil on canvas
155 x 186
1998

THE BALLET DANCERS

Caught in their measured dance,
we understand that deepest love
is just a bending of bodies towards each other.
A brief interlacing of uplifted arms.
Anger and disdain
show in the skilled pointing of a toe.
Tragedy is no more
than a long parting of fingertips.
Death itself is an arched body,
slowly subsiding into silk and lace.

Seagulls, Saltee Islands
oil on board
61 x 76
2004

MONK'S ISLAND

On all his travels he searched for plants,
seeds, saplings, cuttings of all kinds,
each one a collector's cherished joy,
to bring back to his island on the Shannon.
Being a knowledgeable and careful gardener,
all he planted there took root and flourished.

Dove-tree, myrtle, giant fern, acacia,
grew beside the native pine and willow.
Layered shrubs of oriental blossom
sheltered the nesting ducks.
Musky scent from ginger lilies filled the air,
blending with the honey smell of gorse.

Like the plants, his contentment grew
as the enchanted island shaped itself around him.
At night, rowing far out into the lake,
he would sing, his voice rising to the moonlit sky,
a powerful chant of glory and thanksgiving,
his boat drifting among reflected stars.

Sea, Ardamine Beach
oil on board
61 x 122
1988

APHRODITE RISING

The scene is set.
Arms of rock hold the small bay
in a quiet embrace.
Plumes of spray rise from the furthest rock.
The first rays of morning sun
light the white cliffs.

In a warm turquoise sea, ripples spread.
A form shimmers beneath the water,
alabaster face, floating golden hair,
slowly breaks the surface.
As Aphrodite rises, the sun grows in light.

She stands, water courses down her body.
Glowing drops follow her perfect shape.
She looks at this new world, cheeks flushed,
lips parted in delight and wonderment.
She puts one small foot onto the pebbled beach
and in that moment make the land immortal.

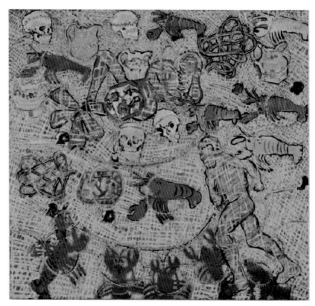

Skeletons and Lobsters
oil on canvas
183 x 244
2006

THE SCREEN

War on television is remote
even though the camera rests
on faces torn by fear and loss,
it is still a foreign land.

Sometimes it is only the trees
standing broken at the edge of the screen,
blackened, snapped like missing limbs,
that can speak to you.

Even worse is the untouched tree
in full bloom over twisted bodies
and you think
there is a tree like that in my garden.

Self Portrait in Yellow
oil on canvas
41 x 26
2014

MEMOIR

Autobiography
is names and places,
facts needing accurate research.
The sectioning of one's life
into manageable parts,
childhood, marriage, career.
Double checking on a life.

Sitting now in this still room,
knowing the view outside the window,
a vase of flowers on a familiar table,
one photograph, perhaps a letter.
Associations linking up like dominoes,
these bring me all that is important
to know what matters most about my life.

Boats, Rio de Janeiro
oil on canvas
92 x 122
2014

PISCES

At its edge the lake is full of light.
Sun shafts through shallow water
showing rocks, grey-brown and orange,
eddies of sand rise where small fish stir.

We pole the boats through thick reeds,
long anchor-stems of lilies brush the sides.
Our fishing rods are upright like slender masts.
We reach the open water, here the colours change,
deep-green, opaque, flecked with tiny flies.
We cast out lines, the water quickly takes,
stretching them out behind us as we move.
The silver spoon baits, turning, beating,
pulse their steady rhythm through our hands.

Our lines sink deep into another world,
down where the monster pike lie waiting,
hovering in their dark weed caverns
with dull eye and jagged evil mouth.
Past them come our dancing silver baits,
armed with bright and deadly hooks,
spinning a path through fathomless dark,
luring, tempting the cannibal fish.
We wait above, in our world serene with sun.

Three Clowns (detail)
oil on board
61 x 112
1983

FACIAL

With my eyes shut I feel her fingers
exploring my face,
temples, eye sockets, cheek bones,
defining the skull beneath my skin.
Then with sweet-smelling creams,
rose, lavender, geranium,
she traces the hills and valleys of my face,
following the paths where tears have flooded.
She smoothes the frown and worry lines,
lifts the downturn corner of my mouth.
She strokes, pats, plays with my face.
Impersonal fingers mimic caresses,
wellsprings of memory are freed,
that surge and set my mind on fire.
But I lie still, I do not break
the placid mask she draws upon my face.

'Caro Mio Ben' (unfinished)
oil on canvas
100 x 41
2013

THE PIANO

The piano played for her childhood,
down distant corridors, through open windows,
trills and scales beating like bird wings,
telling of freedom as yet unknown.

In her mid-life, the piano became riotous,
chuckled and sang, growled in the low notes,
but did it all in such a jazzy manner
that no offence was ever taken.

Her last years were a stately minuet,
with echoes of nostalgic tango.
In highs and lows the piano accompanied her
and finished with a triumphant requiem.

The Blue Bowl
oil on board
30 x 40
2014

THE BLUE BOWL

The bowl comes from Corsica
but it doesn't need the sun
to make it glow with an undreamt of blue.
A simple bowl,
pleasing in shape and size,
deceptive in its innocence.
There is comfort in just holding it.

But more than that –
looking down into it you are lost.
It draws you in, encircles you with blue,
spinning you into its depth,
more profound than the midnight ocean.
This intensity of colour concentrates my thoughts
and gives them back to me.
Acknowledged and transformed.

Trees and Roots
oil on board
76 x 61
2002

FIRESEED

Hardly asleep when the dawn comes,
unyielding in bare, grey light,
I rise reluctantly.
The cold seizes my bones,
outside the blurred shape of cattle wait,
heavy in their dependency.

The shadowy kitchen shows me
cold stone floor and I search
for the one glowing sod of turf
buried deep in the grey ash.
The incandescent seed
which survived the frozen night.

Invincible element of fire,
bursting into nourishment of flame.

May Kirwan
oil on board
46 x 36
1982

COLUMBINE

He wanted to ask her too many questions
but she defeated him.

She took thick white makeup
and put it on her face, all over,
covering every expression line.
On this white mask she drew arching eyebrows,
and black upward strokes on each side of her mouth,
to make a wide, unchanging smile.
When he talked she just looked at him,
no telltale signs of hurt or pain.
Her blank, unsmiling face unreadable, unassailable,
until the impossibility of reaching her
finally destroyed him and he ran.

When he had gone she cleaned her face
and smiled her real smile at the whole world.

Cat with Two Tails
oil on canvas
81 x 66
1995

LITTLE CAT MINNOW

You make your presence known
in shadows flitting across trees.
Small branches tremble, a leaf dances,
or in the ripple moving through tall grass,
invisible jungle cat, it could be you.

I would meet you in unexpected places,
feel your gaze from some high wall,
or coming towards me on a strange path,
aloof, with your Egyptian goddess walk,
night and day, sun and moon your friends.

Later you chose a sunlit window
or the glowing warmth of winter fires
curled in the deep intensity of sleep,
my lap no longer scorned became a haven.
Your purring the sound of peace.

Now your brave spirit is free to roam
in all the places you love the best.
Little cat, beautiful and brave,
I knew and loved you, but never solved
the mystery in your jewel-bright eyes.

Hands, detail *Woman with Breasts*
oil on canvas
183 x 153
2004

SIGN LANGUAGE

You said to me very seriously,
we must buy a hand made out of wood.
You had seen one advertised,
each finger jointed, movable wrist,
to stand between us as an interpreter.

Michelangelo had one, you told me,
fortune-tellers and magicians use them.
All your emotions can be expressed
– fear, anger, love, desire –
in just how you set the fingers.

I hoped you were joking.
I wanted to talk to you by leaning forward,
whispering in your ear.
Letting your hair brush my cheek,
feeling the warmth of your skin.

How could this wooden ornament
be some magical mediator?
Its talent is sign language.
Do you think it could bridge
all that is unspoken between us?

Man Saluting Giraffe Man
oil on canvas
214 x 244
2006

OLD MAN OF ARAN

He was forty years in America,
came home to see his brother die,
stayed on in his parents' cottage.
At eighty he still worked the fields,
walked to do his shopping once a week,
returned with a sack over his shoulder.
Only the white statue in the window welcomed him.
He had never married.
He knew that the single dry-stone wall
took more art in building than the double,
which could lean against other stones.
He was content.
He watched the swans nesting,
the seals playing on the rocks below.
Before him the Atlantic swept uncluttered to America.
He had been there, and now was home.

Crocodiles, Dublin Zoo
oil on board
61 x 76
1999

THE EIGHTIETH BIRTHDAY PRESENT

My aunt was given as her eightieth birthday present
a trip through the Florida mangrove swamps.
She took it as a compliment to her fortitude
and accepted with pride.

I like to think of her
dressed in whatever one wears for mangrove swamps,
getting eagerly into that boat, hiding her stiffness,
sitting bolt upright on the wooden seat, missing nothing,
as they sail past swimming crocodiles
into the half-lit murmuring shadows of the swamp.

Would she have had binoculars?
Or could one see far enough into this murky world?
Silent, except for far-off muted cries,
birds perhaps, or strange swamp creatures.
Otherwise there was only the lap of tidal waters,
the occasional rush of bubbles rising like a sigh.
They steered between gnarled amphibious trees,
mis-shapen trunks knee-deep in water,
draped in vines and Spanish moss,
looking like fierce old men in tattered clothes.
Here and there, snakes lay along branches,
water moccasins opening their white silent mouths
watching, as my aunt passed slowly by.

I picture her coming home,
at this point admitting that she was tired,
but rejoicing that in her long life
one more unexpected landmark had been safely passed.

Yellow Milk Churn
oil on board
122 x 81
2008

Holiday with Norah

We knew every turn in the road that led
to your white farmhouse at the lake's edge.
You would be standing at the open door,
your welcome as warm as the glowing turf fire.

To us children your house was magic.
We slept in two brass beds, set end to end,
the windows, wide open to the sweet air
brought in the twilight rustling hens.
'I hung a lantern for you', you said,
and we looked out together at the moon
sailing high over the still lake.

Everyday we feasted at the kitchen table –
bacon, cut from the side, hung in smokey rafters.
Eggs, new laid, brown bread from the turf oven,
your own butter, apple tarts and cream.
We did not think of those cold early mornings
when you milked the Kerry cow who kicked
– the milky cross you drew on her side
was a prayer for safety and thanksgiving –
you would separate the thick cream,
and work the churn, over and under, till butter came.
Every drop of water you carried from the well,
icy-cold, iron tasting, in heavy silver buckets.
The every day and every week of labour
were poured out for us in shining plenty.

And we, happy, loved, replete,
believed you lived in paradise.

Haycocks from Nursery (detail)
oil on board
46 x 61
1992

HAYMAKING

The hay is saved,
bales stacked sweet smelling in the high barn,
secure for bare winter days.
Tonight we are dancing,
kitchen swept clean, the fire blazing
a barrel of porter, and Jack, the fiddler,
setting the room in motion,
jigs and reels, feet stamping the stone floor.

I had seen you in the hay fields,
a stranger, taller and browner than other men,
bare-chested, working twice as hard as they.
You never saw me, but now you look.
I dance near, letting my skirt brush your body.
That is the limit of my daring.
But you hold me, we are in the reel,
Close, then far away, in the pattern of the dance.

Tomorrow when the kitchen is cold and empty,
I shall find one glowing piece of turf
hidden far down under the white ash.
I shall take it up, build dry pieces around it,
and blow so gently, hoping and hoping
that the small spark will blossom into fire.

Lifebuoy with Nets and Rocks
oil on canvas
91 x 112
2010

SEA OF GLASS

The sea stretches so still under the sun
the only movement is at its edge,
no more than a gentle stroking of the white beach.

Looking down, the separate colours of the sea
show themselves,
distinct bands of bright blue, then green,
soft brown and sudden turquoise,
caught in the slanting sun,
pale sands makes the shallow water gleam.

It is a rare moment of stillness
like those few times in life
when one can feel with perfect clarity,
completeness,
held in a fragile balance of air and light.

About the Author
CLEMENCY EMMET

I was born in London to an Irish father and an American mother, who gave to my older sister Pamela and me a most happy childhood. We travelled widely as my father was in the Diplomatic Service. We spent the longest time in Denmark which we all loved, until the country was invaded in 1940. Luckily all the diplomats and their families were sent home safely to their different countries. My youngest sister Rosemary was born in Ireland. My mother then took us all on to America, while my father went back to work for the war effort in London. We spent three years in California until the war ended and my father came to get us. We then had an epic drive across America taking the shortest possible way as petrol was still strictly rationed. New York was crowded with returning soldiers and it wasn't until January when at last we were able to get on to a 'Liberty Ship' as it was called then. My father had to go ahead of us as he was needed in Denmark. On our ship there were two flimsy huts built on the top open deck, one for war correspondents, the other for us. It was a very bad crossing with rough and stormy weather, where the waves would break over the deck and sea water would rush in around our beds. It took us two and a half weeks to cross the Atlantic but we finally reached Sweden and took a train south to Denmark where my father was waiting for us with a car and a large hamper of delicious food, it was a very happy moment! The joy of being back in Denmark was overwhelming for all of us. There we spent four very happy years. I then went, in my father's footsteps, to Trinity College Dublin, reading 'Modern Languages' which I loved. It was at Trinity that I first started writing poetry. At that time I met my beloved husband James Emmet, direct descendent of United Irishman Thomas Addis Emmet, and older brother of the patriot Robert Emmet. We have lived in Ireland ever since, farming first in County Wexford and then in County Wicklow. My son now looks after the family land and woods organically. My daughter also lives close by. I have four grandchildren. All the family are a great inspiration and encouragement to me in every way. I do hope you will enjoy this collection of my poems.

About the Artist
ELIZABETH COPE

'When I was nine years old, my sister came home from Paris with a box of paints. It was the smell of the oil paints that seduced me into becoming a painter'. Elizabeth Cope has exhibited for many years with the Solomon Gallery, Dublin. Her recent one man shows include the National Arts Club, New York, 2012; Jacques Lamy Gallery, Dallas, Texas, 2012; the Spitalfields Gallery, London, 2013; and Galerie Instituto Volusiano, Sao Paulo, 2014. She has been invited to exhibit her Brazilian paintings in October 2014 at the Origin Gallery, Fitzwilliam Street, Dublin. In 2015 a monograph of her paintings will be published by Gandon Editions. She is represented in Dallas at Jacques Lamy Gallery. Elizabeth Cope is honoured and delighted to collaborate with Clemency Emmet in her book of beautiful poetry.

ACKNOWLEDGEMENTS

It is with warm appreciation and very many thanks to Elizabeth Cope for enhancing my poems so beautifully with her most lovely paintings and indeed for helping me to get this collection of poems together. I am so grateful to Gillian Somerville-Large for writing her very kind 'Foreword'.

The Three Graces by the Sea
oil on canvas
41 x 61
2013